ILLUMINATION PRESENTS

THE SECRET LIFE OF

PeTs ™

ALL ABOUT THE PETS AND ME!

centum

THE SECRET LIFE OF PETS: ALL ABOUT THE PETS AND ME!
A CENTUM BOOK
HARDBACK 9781910916551

Published in Great Britain by Centum Books Ltd

This edition published 2016
© 2016 Universal Studios Licensing LLC.

1 3 5 7 9 10 8 6 4 2

UNIVERSAL.

Centum Books Ltd, 20 Devon Square, Newton Abbot, Devon, TQ12 2HR, UK
books@centumbooksltd.co.uk

CENTUM BOOKS Limited Reg. No. 07641486

A CIP catalogue record for this book is available from the British Library

Printed in China.

WELCOME!

THIS BOOK **BELONGS TO:**

_____

Have you ever wondered what your pets do when you're not at home? Do they sit at the door and wait until you come home? Do they have adventures of their own or watch TV and practise looking cute?

In this book, you can learn all about your favourite characters from **THE SECRET LIFE OF PETS** and fill in your own details, secrets and favourite things – as well as your pet's.

How many times can you FIND a bone hidden in this book?

Meet
THE PETS

In a New York apartment block live a group of pets.
LET'S MEET THEM ALL!

Duke

Max

Gidget

Chloe

Buddy

Mel

Norman

Pops

Tiberius

Leonard

Sweetpea

ALL ABOUT ME

MY NAME IS _____

MY BIRTHDAY IS _____

I AM _____ YEARS OLD

I WAS BORN IN _____

MY HAIR COLOUR IS _____

MY EYE COLOUR IS _____

MY HEIGHT IS _____

MY SHOE SIZE IS _____

MY PET IS CALLED _____

DRAW YOURSELF
AND YOUR PET IN THE BOX BELOW:

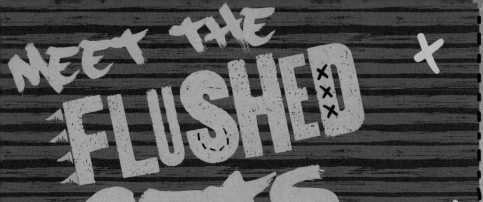

MEET THE FLUSHED PETS

THE FLUSHED PETS ARE A GANG OF STREET PETS, LED BY THEIR CRAZED LEADER – SNOWBALL. LET'S MEET THEM ALL!

SNOWBALL

TATTOO

LIBERATED FOREVER! DOMESTICATED NEVER!

DERICK

OZONE

RIPPER

DRAGON

11

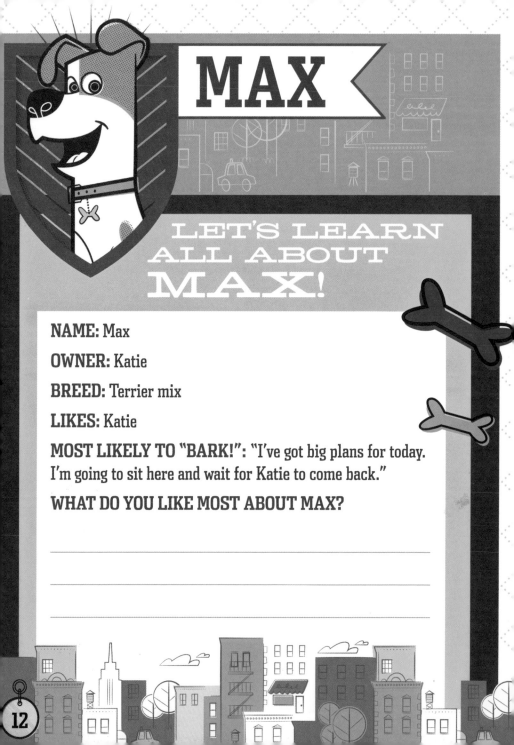

MAX

LET'S LEARN ALL ABOUT MAX!

NAME: Max

OWNER: Katie

BREED: Terrier mix

LIKES: Katie

MOST LIKELY TO "BARK!": "I've got big plans for today. I'm going to sit here and wait for Katie to come back."

WHAT DO YOU LIKE MOST ABOUT MAX?

WHERE IS MY
COLLAR?

Can you draw a collar on each of these pets?

ALL ABOUT **MY** PET

A pet is everyone's best friend – they're always so loving and loyal. Use this page to fill in everything about your pet.

My pet's name is _____

My pet's birthday is _____

My pet is _____ years old

My pet is a _____

My pet's fur/skin/feather colour is _____

My pet's favourite treat is _____

My pet's favourite thing to do is _____

What I love most about my pet is _____

_____

_____

DRAW YOUR PET IN THE BOX BELOW:

DUKE

PET SOCIETY

ORDER OF · THE PAW

LET'S LEARN ALL ABOUT DUKE!

NAME: Duke

OWNER: Katie

BREED: Mutt

LIKES: Sausages

MOST LIKELY TO "BARK!": "If it's gonna come down to you or me, it's gonna be me."

WHAT DO YOU LIKE MOST ABOUT DUKE?

PETS AND OWNERS:
SOULMATES!

There's nothing like the love between an owner and their pet.
DOODLE some special moments of you and your pets together
or STICK SOME PHOTOS below.

HOW TO
CARE FOR YOUR
PET

Whether you have a loving PUPPY, a cute CAT or an adorable BUNNY, it's important to look after your best friend. Here are a few tips to keep your pet happy.

Make sure your pet always has fresh, clean WATER.

Make sure your pet eats HEALTHY food.

Always make time to PLAY with and exercise your pet.

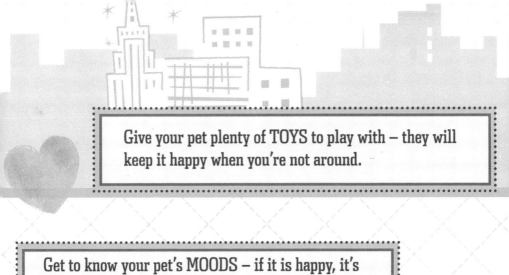

Give your pet plenty of TOYS to play with – they will keep it happy when you're not around.

Get to know your pet's MOODS – if it is happy, it's playtime; if it is sleepy, let it sleep; if it is sad, give it a hug.

BRUSH, WASH and CLEAN your pet, so it looks good and feels great!

GIDGET

LET'S LEARN ALL ABOUT GIDGET!

NAME: Gidget

BREED: Pomeranian

LIKES: Max

MOST LIKELY TO "BARK!": "If you find Max, I'll be your best friend."

WHAT DO YOU LIKE MOST ABOUT GIDGET?

_____

_____

_____

_____

HOW **MANY** SAUSAGES?

Max and Duke know they can never have too many sausages.
HOW MANY sausages can you count on this page?

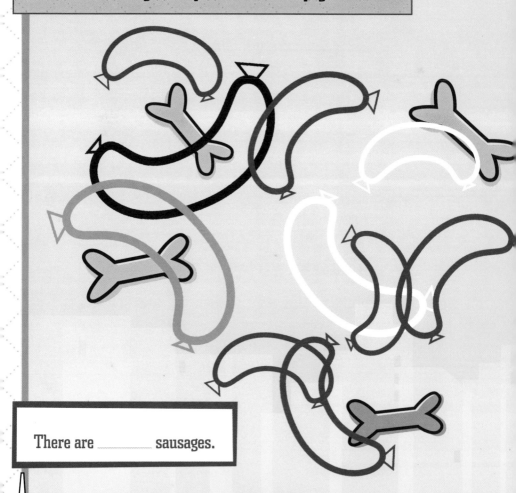

There are _____ sausages.

Can you find 5 hidden bones, too?

SAUSAGE FACTORY

WHICH PET ARE YOU?

Take this quiz to find out!

STAR!

Do you have long, unruly hair?

YES

Are you good at making new friends?

YES

Do you always solve problems for your friends?

NO

YES

NO

Do you have a favourite ball?

YES

Do you look cute on the outside, but inside you're 100% tough?

NO

Is your favourite TV show a soap opera?

NO

NO

Do you have a secret crush on someone?

YES

Do you love handbags?

YES

Do you have dark hair?

YES

YES

NO

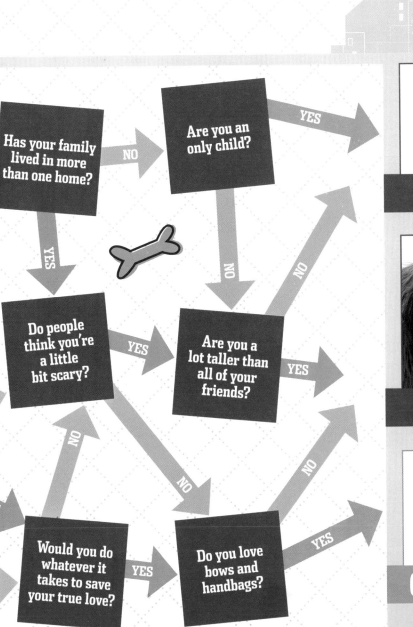

Has your family lived in more than one home?

NO → Are you an only child?

YES → MAX

Are you an only child? **NO** →

YES → Do people think you're a little bit scary?

Do people think you're a little bit scary? **YES** → Are you a lot taller than all of your friends?

NO →

Are you a lot taller than all of your friends? **YES** →

NO →

Would you do whatever it takes to save your true love? **YES** → Do you love bows and handbags?

Do you love bows and handbags? **YES** →

MAX

DUKE

GIDGET

SNOWBALL

LET'S LEARN ALL ABOUT

SNOWBALL!

NAME: SNOWBALL

BREED: RABBIT

LIVES: IN THE UNDERBELLY

MOST LIKELY TO SAY: "LIBERATED FOREVER! DOMESTICATED NEVER!"

WHAT DO YOU THINK IS SNOWBALL'S CRAZIEST PLAN?

_____

_____

_____

_____

OBEY THE BUNNY

BEST
FRIENDS
FOREVER!

When Max meets Duke for the first time, they're not the best of friends. But they're going to need to become friends quickly if they want to find their way back home.

Draw yourself with your best friends (and their pets!) below.

SPOT THE DIFFERENCES

CAN YOU SPOT

10 DIFFERENCES

BETWEEN THESE PICTURES?

34

COLOUR IN
A CARROT FOR
EVERY DIFFERENCE
YOU SPOT.

ANSWERS ON PAGE 93

TATTOO PUZZLE +

CAN YOU MATCH THE MISSING PIECES OF THIS PUZZLE TO THEIR CORRECT POSITION?

A

B

C

D

E

DRAW TATTOO'S TATTOOS

UH, OH! THIS PICTURE OF TATTOO
IS MISSING HIS TATTOOS.
CAN YOU DRAW THEM IN PLACE?

X X X

PET ESSENTIALS

When Katie brings home Duke to her apartment, he can't believe his luck! He is finally in a comfortable home full of love and everything a dog could ever want!
Here is a list of pet essentials you'll need to keep your pet happy!

PET FOOD

Make sure you always have plenty of FOOD for your pet. Make sure it's tasty and HEALTHY, too.

FOOD AND WATER BOWLS

Make sure your pet always has access to FRESH WATER. Place it's food and water in the same place in the house.

TOYS

Provide toys to keep your pet ENTERTAINED.

BED

Provide your pet with a safe and comfy place to SLEEP. As Duke and Max know, if you have more than one pet make sure they each have their own place to sleep so there are no arguments!

KEEP YOUR PET FIT

If your pet is a dog, make sure you take it on walks. If you have another pet, ask your vet for tips on how to keep your pet FIT and ACTIVE.

MOST IMPORTANTLY...
GIVE YOUR PET
LOTS OF LOVE!

PET NAME GENERATOR!

The first thing you do to welcome a pet to the family is give it a name. Use this name generator to create your next pet's name.

For the FIRST NAME, take your pet's birth date.
For the MIDDLE NAME, take your age.
For the SURNAME, just use your own surname!

BOY	GIRL
1. Max	1. Gidget
2. Duke	2. Chloe
3. Leonard	3. Rita
4. Pops	4. Cookie
5. Tiberius	5. Lady
6. Norman	6. Coco
7. Buddy	7. Luna
8. Arnold	8. Lucky
9. Blue	9. Nala
10. Rocky	10. Ruby

1. Pawson
2. Wiggles
3. Fluffington
4. Chewy
5. Gizmo
6. Woofles
7. Miewton
8. Nibbles
9. Schmoozipoo
10. Waddles

My pet's name is _____

If your pet's birth date or name letters come to more than ten, add the numbers together until you have one number.

For example: 29 is 2 + 9 = 11, 1 + 1 = 2.

MY FAMILY TREE

Pets are an important part of any family.
Fill in your family tree on these pages –
DON'T FORGET TO INCLUDE YOUR PETS!

My mum
_____

My sibling
_____

A photo of
your family

Me
_____

My sibling
_____

My dad
_____

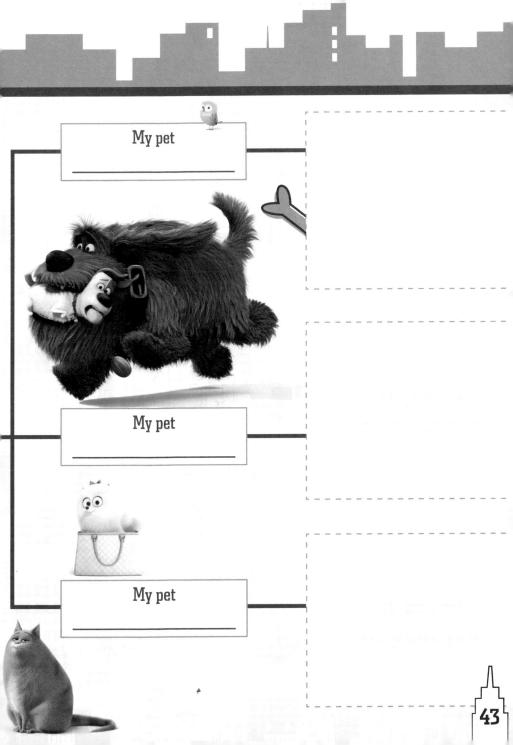

My pet
_____

My pet
_____

My pet
_____

IT'S TIME FOR MY
CLOSE-UP!

Can you recognise any of these pets from their CLOSE-UPS?

1

2

3

4

5

6

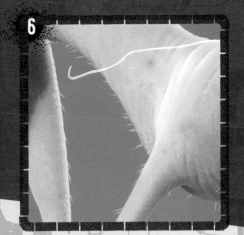

7

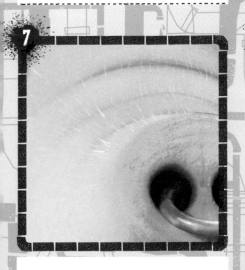

8

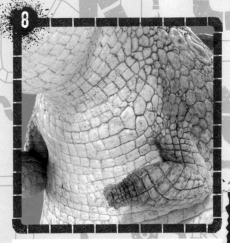

ANSWERS ON PAGE 93

NO BARK...
JUST BITE

COLOURING

Colour in these pictures of Max and Chloe.

WHERE'S
NORMAN?

This guinea pig is lost in the apartment block's vents.
Can you draw him a path through them?

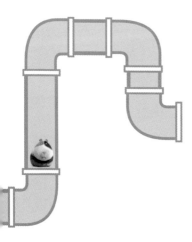

ATTITUDE TO SPARE

OBEY THE BUNNY

LIBERATED

FOREVER! DOMESTICATED NEVER!

THIS IS MY HAPPY FACE

INSANELY CUTE ALSO INSANE

OBEY THE BUNNY

49

Untangle

THE LEADS

It's been a fun day at the dog park. The dogs were so excited, they've got their leads tangled! Can you help to UNRAVEL them and find out whose lead is whose?

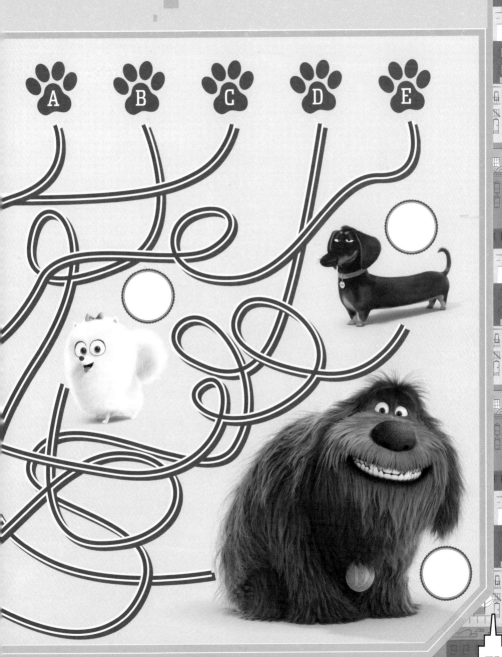

SAUSAGE
PEOPLE

It's doggie heaven – sausages as far as the eye can see. Ignore the rumbles of your tummy and see if you can answer the questions below.

CIRCLE all the sausages who are wearing buns and COUNT them.

There are _____ sausages wearing buns.

DRAW AN X on all the sausages with mustard hair and COUNT them.

There are _____ sausages with mustard hair.

DRAW A DOT on all the sausages wearing pickle skirts and COUNT them.

There are _____ sausages wearing pickle skirts.

AUSAGE FACTORY

Are there more sausages with mustard hair or more sausages wearing buns?

SQUARES
X GAME

HOW TO PLAY:

✗ Take turns drawing a line between any two side-by-side dots.
The player who draws the fourth line that makes a square, conquers that square, marks it with their initials (please don't mark your square territory how dogs would!), then takes another turn.

✗ Once all the squares that can be made have been completed, the player with the most squares marked with their initials **WINS** and is **'TOP DOG'** for the rest of the day!

SNOWBALL'S

START 1

UNDERGROUND
MAZE

START 2

START 3

CAN YOU PICK A PATH THROUGH THIS TRICKY MAZE,
WHICH PASSES BY EACH OF THE FLUSHED PETS?

WHICH START
DO YOU NEED TO USE TO FIND ALL THE FLUSHED PETS?

FINISH

ANSWERS ON PAGE 94

HOW MANY CARROTS DID YOU FIND ON YOUR ROUTE? _____

57

DOG PARK
DIFFERENCES

It's a lovely, sunny day – the perfect day for a walk in the dog park.

CAN YOU SPOT 10 DIFFERENCES BETWEEN THESE 2 PICTURES?

Answers on page 94

DOG TO
HUMAN
TRANSLATION

Max is not happy that Duke has moved into his home and he's trying to tell Katie about how he feels.
Can you decode what Max is trying to 'bark' to Katie?

KEY

A	B	C	D	E	F	G	H	I	J
Q	A	X	Z	W	S	E	D	C	R
K	L	M	N	O	P	Q	R	S	T
F	V	T	G	B	Y	H	N	U	J

	U	V	W	X	Y	Z	
	M	I	K	O	L	P	

_ _ _ _ _ _ _ _ _ _ _ _

_ _ _ _ _ ! _ _ ' _ _ _ _ _ _ _ _ _ !

Answers on page 94

PLAN YOUR
PET'S WEEK

There's one simple thing that every pet loves – an exciting week packed with lots of games with their owner.
Use the following pages to plan out your pet's week.

MONDAY

TUESDAY

WEDNESDAY

THURSDAY

FRIDAY

SATURDAY

SUNDAY

PLAN YOUR
PET'S WEEK

Use these pages to plan the ultimate and most exciting week EVER with your pet. What will you do? Walkies up a mountain? Playing fetch at a sports stadium? Or perhaps skydiving? You decide!

MONDAY

TUESDAY

WEDNESDAY

THURSDAY

FRIDAY

SATURDAY

SUNDAY

PLAN A PARTY
FOR YOUR PET!

There's one place in the apartment building that's a party hot-spot – Pops' place! His owner is always away, and he loves to throw parties! Pets shouldn't have to wait until their owner is away to party – why don't you throw a party for your pet?

Here are some tips on planning the perfect party for your pet:

 Invite your human friends too, especially those who also have pets!

 Pick a space where there is plenty of room for all your guests to play and run about – outside is ideal. If it's inside, make sure it's pet friendly (remove all breakable objects!).

 Have lots of balls and toys on hand. That way all humans and pets can play with them and have a great time.

 Make sure there are plenty of cleaning supplies for any accidents that might occur.

 Get a pet cake – that your pets and their four-legged (or more!) guests can eat There are plenty of recipes online so you could make   your own. Always make sure it doesn't contain anything that might give your pet a poorly tummy.

 Don't forget to give each of your guests a goodie bag when they leave. You can fill it with pet treats, toys or perhaps a photo of the fun they've had at your party.

PLAN A PARTY
FOR YOUR PET!

GAMES

Activities are always a **fun** part of any party! Here are some suggestions:

 Set up a pet agility course. Use sticks, stones, chairs or anything else you have handy. Perhaps get the owners to compete, too!

 If you're having a costume party, get everyone to vote for the best pet-owner costume!

 You could also have a pets award show, and award the guest dogs with rosettes for 'Cutest pet', 'Best-trained', 'Funniest pet' and so on. Make sure each guest gets an award so no one feels left out.

DECORATIONS

A fun theme is essential for any good party.
What will the theme for your party be?

Use this space below to plan how you'll decorate
your pet's party!

MY

FAVOURITE THINGS

Gidget has many favourite things: handbags, soap operas and
especially Max! Scribble down your FAVOURITE THINGS
as fast as you can to discover what you're really thinking!

COLOUR

_____

NUMBER

_____

ANIMAL

_____

SEASON

_____

HOBBY

_____

BEST FRIEND

_____

SONG

BOOK

SMELL

DRINK

FOOD

MUSIC GROUP

FLOWER

GAME

FILM

MY PET'S FAVOURITE THINGS

Norman can't remember a lot of things, including where he lives.
Write down your pet's favourite things so you'll never forget them.

FOOD

TOY

PLACE TO BE TICKLED

PLACE TO SLEEP

TREAT

GAME

COLLAR

PLACE TO HIDE THINGS

THING TO DO when they think you aren't watching

These are my FAVOURITE THINGS about my pet

MY BIGGEST SECRETS

Gidget has a secret . . . she has a crush on Max –
don't tell anyone!
Fill in your most secret-est secrets onto these pages and
then place invisible tape along the edges of the pages so
no one will ever notice your hidden pages.

My biggest secret is: _____

_____

_____

My secret dream is: _____

_____

_____

One thing I secretly like is: _____

_____

_____

My secret dream for the future is: _____

_____

_____

I trust this person/pet with all my secrets:

_____

_____

Pets'

QUIZ

How much do you know about the film, *The Secret Life of Pets* and the characters? Test your knowledge by taking this quiz!

1. Which of these pets throws lots of parties?

   a. Pops   b. Max   c. Gidget   d. Snowball

2. Which pet can't remember where he lives?

   a. Sweetpea   b. Tiberius   c. Mel   d. Norman

3. Who has a secret crush on Max?

   a. Duke   b. Snowball   c. Gidget   d. Chloe

4. What is the name of the crocodile from the Flushed Pets?

   a. Derick   b. Ricky   c. Viper   d. Scaly

5. What colour is Max's collar?

6. What is the name of the Flushed Pets' underground lair?

7. Gidget is a bulldog.

8. Chloe does not like cake.

9. Max and Duke live with Katie.

10. Mel loves squirrels.

COLLAR DOODLE

All pets need a collar and tag, so that if they ever get lost, they can be returned home. Fill in all these collar tags with information about your pet, or pets you wish you had!

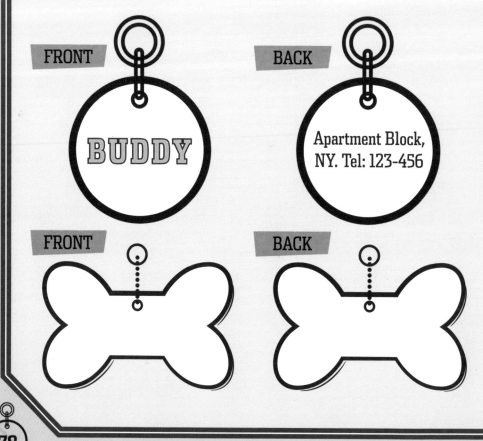

FRONT

BACK

BUDDY

Apartment Block, NY. Tel: 123-456

FRONT

BACK

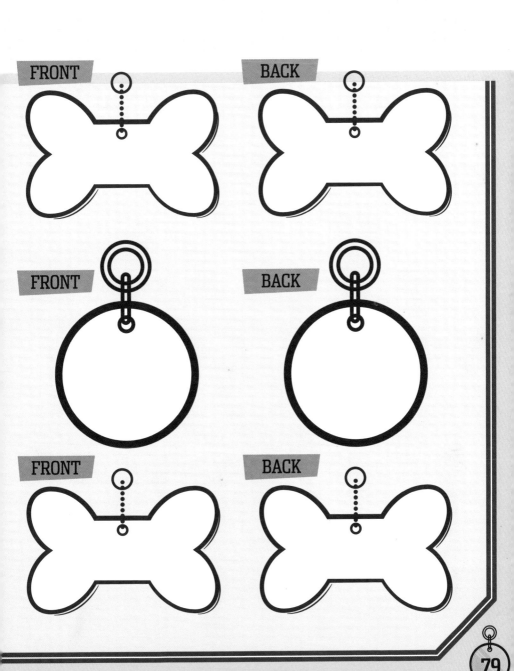

FRONT BACK

FRONT BACK

FRONT BACK

COLOURING

Colour in these pictures of Gidget and Mel.

MEL

81

COPY COLOUR

COPY THIS PICTURE of the FLUSHED PETS INTO THE GRID OPPOSITE.

FLUSHED PETS

DON'T FORGET TO
COLOUR THEM IN!

MY PET'S DIARY

There's one thing for certain – Max, Duke, Gidget and the rest of the pets go on an amazing adventure!
Write about any adventures you and your pet go on together – no event is too big or too small, so get creative!

Perhaps you can fill this page with what you imagine your pet gets up to when you aren't home.

MY FRIENDS AND ME

FILL THESE PAGES WITH PICTURES OF
YOURSELF AND
YOUR FRIENDS.

ANSWERS

PAGE 26–27
There are 24 sausages.

PAGE 35

PAGE 36
The missing puzzle pieces are pieces B, C and D.

PAGE 44–45
1-Max, 2-Duke, 3-Gidget,
4-Chole, 5-Snowball, 6-Ozone,
7-Tattoo, 8-Derick.

PAGE 50–51
A-Buddy, B-Duke, C-Gidget,
D-Mel, E-Max.

PAGE 52–53
- There are **4** sausages
  wearing buns.
- There are **8** sausages
  with mustard hair.
- There are **5** sausages
  wearing pickle skirts.

There are more sausages
with mustard hair.

ANSWERS

PAGE 56-57

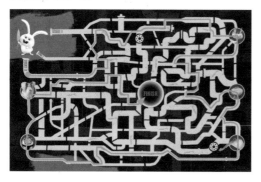

PAGE 58-59

PAGE 60-61
DUKE HAS EATEN ALL
MY FOOD! I'M HUNGRY!

PAGE 76-77
1. a. Pops
2. d. Norman
3. c. Gidget
4. a. Derick
5. blue
6. The Underbelly

True or false?
7. false
8. false
9. true
10. false